This journal belongs to:

Kindness
Scavenger Hunt

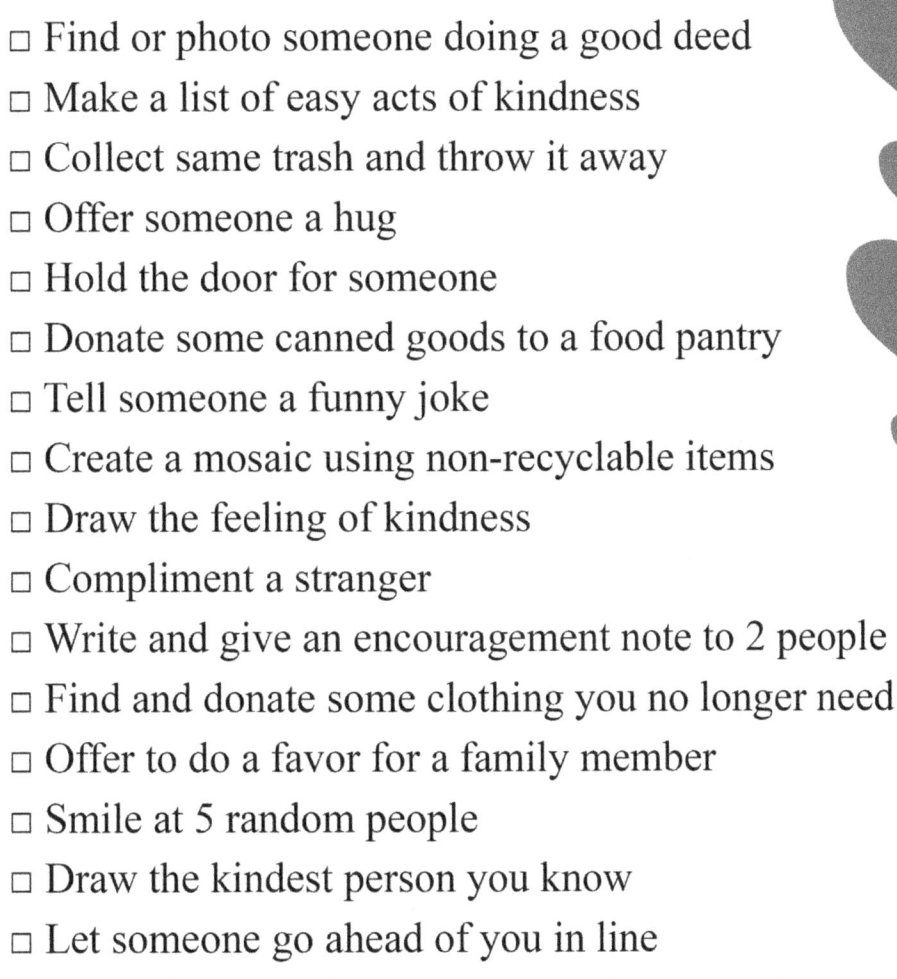

- ☐ Find or photo someone doing a good deed
- ☐ Make a list of easy acts of kindness
- ☐ Collect same trash and throw it away
- ☐ Offer someone a hug
- ☐ Hold the door for someone
- ☐ Donate some canned goods to a food pantry
- ☐ Tell someone a funny joke
- ☐ Create a mosaic using non-recyclable items
- ☐ Draw the feeling of kindness
- ☐ Compliment a stranger
- ☐ Write and give an encouragement note to 2 people
- ☐ Find and donate some clothing you no longer need
- ☐ Offer to do a favor for a family member
- ☐ Smile at 5 random people
- ☐ Draw the kindest person you know
- ☐ Let someone go ahead of you in line
- ☐ Make flowers using non-recyclable materials
- ☐ Give the flowers to friends
- ☐ Share a memory with a loved one

- Acts of Kindness Tracker -

Recipient:

What I did:

Why I did it:

How they responded:

How it made me feel:

I am inspired to:

An act of kindness I saw today:

DATE

TIME

Additional Notes or Drawings:

Recipient:

What I did:

Why I did it:

How they responded:

How it made me feel:

I am inspired to:

An act of kindness I saw today:

Additional Notes or Drawings:

DATE

TIME

Recipient:

What I did:

Why I did it:

How they responded:

How it made me feel:

I am inspired to:

An act of kindness I saw today:

DATE

TIME

Additional Notes or Drawings:

Recipient:

What I did:

Why I did it:

How they responded:

How it made me feel:

I am inspired to:

An act of kindness I saw today:

DATE

TIME

Additional Notes or Drawings:

Recipient:

What I did:

Why I did it:

DATE

TIME

How they responded:

How it made me feel:

I am inspired to:

An act of kindness I saw today:

Additional Notes or Drawings:

Recipient:

What I did:

Why I did it:

How they responded:

How it made me feel:

I am inspired to:

An act of kindness I saw today:

Additional Notes or Drawings:

DATE

TIME

Recipient:

What I did:

Why I did it:

How they responded:

How it made me feel:

I am inspired to:

An act of kindness I saw today:

DATE

TIME

Additional Notes or Drawings:

Recipient:

What I did:

Why I did it:

How they responded:

How it made me feel:

I am inspired to:

An act of kindness I saw today:

Additional Notes or Drawings:

DATE

TIME

Recipient:

What I did:

Why I did it:

How they responded:

How it made me feel:

I am inspired to:

An act of kindness I saw today:

Additional Notes or Drawings:

DATE

TIME

Recipient:

What I did:

Why I did it:

How they responded:

How it made me feel:

I am inspired to:

An act of kindness I saw today:

Additional Notes or Drawings:

DATE

TIME

Recipient:

What I did:

Why I did it:

How they responded:

How it made me feel:

I am inspired to:

An act of kindness I saw today:

DATE

TIME

Additional Notes or Drawings:

Recipient:

What I did:

Why I did it:

How they responded:

How it made me feel:

I am inspired to:

An act of kindness I saw today:

DATE

TIME

Additional Notes or Drawings:

Recipient:

What I did:

Why I did it:

How they responded:

How it made me feel:

I am inspired to:

An act of kindness I saw today:

DATE

TIME

Additional Notes or Drawings:

Recipient:

What I did:

Why I did it:

How they responded:

How it made me feel:

I am inspired to:

An act of kindness I saw today:

DATE

TIME

Additional Notes or Drawings:

Recipient:

What I did:

Why I did it:

How they responded:

How it made me feel:

I am inspired to:

An act of kindness I saw today:

Additional Notes or Drawings:

DATE

TIME

Recipient: _____

DATE

What I did: _____

TIME

Why I did it: _____

How they responded: _____

How it made me feel: _____

I am inspired to: _____

An act of kindness I saw today: _____

Additional Notes or Drawings:

Recipient:

What I did:

Why I did it:

How they responded:

How it made me feel:

I am inspired to:

An act of kindness I saw today:

Additional Notes or Drawings:

DATE

TIME

Recipient:

What I did:

Why I did it:

How they responded:

How it made me feel:

I am inspired to:

An act of kindness I saw today:

DATE

TIME

Additional Notes or Drawings:

Recipient:

What I did:

Why I did it:

How they responded:

How it made me feel:

I am inspired to:

An act of kindness I saw today:

Additional Notes or Drawings:

DATE

TIME

Recipient:

What I did:

Why I did it:

How they responded:

How it made me feel:

I am inspired to:

An act of kindness I saw today:

Additional Notes or Drawings:

DATE

TIME

Recipient:

What I did:

Why I did it:

How they responded:

How it made me feel:

I am inspired to:

An act of kindness I saw today:

Additional Notes or Drawings:

DATE

TIME

Recipient:

What I did:

Why I did it:

How they responded:

How it made me feel:

I am inspired to:

An act of kindness I saw today:

Additional Notes or Drawings:

DATE

TIME

Recipient:

What I did:

Why I did it:

DATE

TIME

How they responded:

How it made me feel:

I am inspired to:

An act of kindness I saw today:

Additional Notes or Drawings:

Recipient:

What I did:

Why I did it:

How they responded:

How it made me feel:

I am inspired to:

An act of kindness I saw today:

DATE

TIME

Additional Notes or Drawings:

Recipient:

What I did:

Why I did it:

How they responded:

How it made me feel:

I am inspired to:

An act of kindness I saw today:

DATE

TIME

Additional Notes or Drawings:

Recipient:

What I did:

Why I did it:

How they responded:

How it made me feel:

I am inspired to:

An act of kindness I saw today:

DATE

TIME

Additional Notes or Drawings:

Recipient:

What I did:

Why I did it:

How they responded:

How it made me feel:

I am inspired to:

An act of kindness I saw today:

DATE

TIME

Additional Notes or Drawings:

Recipient:

What I did:

Why I did it:

How they responded:

How it made me feel:

I am inspired to:

An act of kindness I saw today:

Additional Notes or Drawings:

DATE

TIME

Recipient:

What I did:

Why I did it:

DATE

TIME

How they responded:

How it made me feel:

I am inspired to:

An act of kindness I saw today:

Additional Notes or Drawings:

Recipient:

What I did:

Why I did it:

How they responded:

How it made me feel:

I am inspired to:

An act of kindness I saw today:

DATE

TIME

Additional Notes or Drawings:

Recipient:

What I did:

Why I did it:

How they responded:

How it made me feel:

I am inspired to:

An act of kindness I saw today:

DATE

TIME

Additional Notes or Drawings:

Recipient:

What I did:

Why I did it:

How they responded:

How it made me feel:

I am inspired to:

An act of kindness I saw today:

Additional Notes or Drawings:

DATE

TIME

Recipient:

What I did:

Why I did it:

How they responded:

How it made me feel:

I am inspired to:

An act of kindness I saw today:

DATE

TIME

Additional Notes or Drawings:

Recipient:

What I did:

Why I did it:

How they responded:

How it made me feel:

I am inspired to:

An act of kindness I saw today:

Additional Notes or Drawings:

DATE

TIME

Recipient:

What I did:

Why I did it:

DATE

TIME

How they responded:

How it made me feel:

I am inspired to:

An act of kindness I saw today:

Additional Notes or Drawings:

Recipient:

What I did:

Why I did it:

How they responded:

How it made me feel:

I am inspired to:

An act of kindness I saw today:

Additional Notes or Drawings:

DATE

TIME

Recipient:

What I did:

Why I did it:

How they responded:

How it made me feel:

I am inspired to:

An act of kindness I saw today:

Additional Notes or Drawings:

DATE

TIME

Recipient:

What I did:

Why I did it:

How they responded:

How it made me feel:

I am inspired to:

An act of kindness I saw today:

DATE

TIME

Additional Notes or Drawings:

Recipient:

What I did:

Why I did it:

How they responded:

How it made me feel:

I am inspired to:

An act of kindness I saw today:

DATE

TIME

Additional Notes or Drawings:

Recipient:

What I did:

Why I did it:

How they responded:

How it made me feel:

I am inspired to:

An act of kindness I saw today:

DATE

TIME

Additional Notes or Drawings:

Recipient:

What I did:

Why I did it:

How they responded:

How it made me feel:

I am inspired to:

An act of kindness I saw today:

Additional Notes or Drawings:

DATE

TIME

Recipient:

What I did:

Why I did it:

How they responded:

How it made me feel:

I am inspired to:

An act of kindness I saw today:

DATE

TIME

Additional Notes or Drawings:

Recipient:

What I did:

Why I did it:

How they responded:

How it made me feel:

I am inspired to:

An act of kindness I saw today:

DATE

TIME

Additional Notes or Drawings:

Recipient:

What I did:

Why I did it:

How they responded:

How it made me feel:

I am inspired to:

An act of kindness I saw today:

Additional Notes or Drawings:

DATE

TIME

Recipient:

What I did:

Why I did it:

How they responded:

How it made me feel:

I am inspired to:

An act of kindness I saw today:

Additional Notes or Drawings:

DATE

TIME

Recipient:

What I did:

Why I did it:

How they responded:

How it made me feel:

I am inspired to:

An act of kindness I saw today:

Additional Notes or Drawings:

DATE

TIME

Recipient:

What I did:

Why I did it:

How they responded:

How it made me feel:

I am inspired to:

An act of kindness I saw today:

DATE

TIME

Additional Notes or Drawings:

Recipient:

What I did:

Why I did it:

How they responded:

How it made me feel:

I am inspired to:

An act of kindness I saw today:

Additional Notes or Drawings:

DATE

TIME

Recipient:

What I did:

Why I did it:

How they responded:

How it made me feel:

I am inspired to:

An act of kindness I saw today:

Additional Notes or Drawings:

DATE

TIME

Recipient:

What I did:

Why I did it:

How they responded:

How it made me feel:

I am inspired to:

An act of kindness I saw today:

DATE

TIME

Additional Notes or Drawings:

Recipient:

What I did:

Why I did it:

How they responded:

How it made me feel:

I am inspired to:

An act of kindness I saw today:

DATE

TIME

Additional Notes or Drawings:

Recipient:

What I did:

Why I did it:

How they responded:

How it made me feel:

I am inspired to:

An act of kindness I saw today:

DATE

TIME

Additional Notes or Drawings:

Recipient:

What I did:

Why I did it:

How they responded:

How it made me feel:

I am inspired to:

An act of kindness I saw today:

Additional Notes or Drawings:

DATE

TIME

Recipient:

What I did:

Why I did it:

How they responded:

How it made me feel:

I am inspired to:

An act of kindness I saw today:

DATE

TIME

Additional Notes or Drawings:

Recipient:

What I did:

Why I did it:

DATE

TIME

How they responded:

How it made me feel:

I am inspired to:

An act of kindness I saw today:

Additional Notes or Drawings:

Recipient:

What I did:

Why I did it:

How they responded:

How it made me feel:

I am inspired to:

An act of kindness I saw today:

DATE

TIME

Additional Notes or Drawings:

Recipient:

What I did:

Why I did it:

How they responded:

How it made me feel:

I am inspired to:

An act of kindness I saw today:

Additional Notes or Drawings:

DATE

TIME

Recipient:

What I did:

Why I did it:

How they responded:

How it made me feel:

I am inspired to:

An act of kindness I saw today:

Additional Notes or Drawings:

DATE

TIME

Recipient:

What I did:

Why I did it:

How they responded:

How it made me feel:

I am inspired to:

An act of kindness I saw today:

Additional Notes or Drawings:

DATE

TIME

Recipient:

What I did:

Why I did it:

How they responded:

How it made me feel:

I am inspired to:

An act of kindness I saw today:

Additional Notes or Drawings:

DATE

TIME

Recipient:

What I did:

Why I did it:

How they responded:

How it made me feel:

I am inspired to:

An act of kindness I saw today:

Additional Notes or Drawings:

DATE

TIME

Recipient:

What I did:

Why I did it:

How they responded:

How it made me feel:

I am inspired to:

An act of kindness I saw today:

DATE

TIME

Additional Notes or Drawings:

Recipient:

DATE

What I did:

TIME

Why I did it:

How they responded:

How it made me feel:

I am inspired to:

An act of kindness I saw today:

Additional Notes or Drawings:

Recipient:

What I did:

Why I did it:

How they responded:

How it made me feel:

I am inspired to:

An act of kindness I saw today:

Additional Notes or Drawings:

DATE

TIME

Recipient:

What I did:

Why I did it:

How they responded:

How it made me feel:

I am inspired to:

An act of kindness I saw today:

DATE

TIME

Additional Notes or Drawings:

Recipient:

What I did:

Why I did it:

How they responded:

How it made me feel:

I am inspired to:

An act of kindness I saw today:

Additional Notes or Drawings:

DATE

TIME

Recipient:

What I did:

Why I did it:

How they responded:

How it made me feel:

I am inspired to:

An act of kindness I saw today:

Additional Notes or Drawings:

DATE

TIME

Recipient:

What I did:

Why I did it:

How they responded:

How it made me feel:

I am inspired to:

An act of kindness I saw today:

Additional Notes or Drawings:

DATE

TIME

Recipient:

What I did:

Why I did it:

How they responded:

How it made me feel:

I am inspired to:

An act of kindness I saw today:

Additional Notes or Drawings:

DATE

TIME

Recipient:

What I did:

Why I did it:

How they responded:

How it made me feel:

I am inspired to:

An act of kindness I saw today:

Additional Notes or Drawings:

DATE

TIME

Recipient:

What I did:

Why I did it:

How they responded:

How it made me feel:

I am inspired to:

An act of kindness I saw today:

DATE

TIME

Additional Notes or Drawings:

Recipient:

What I did:

Why I did it:

How they responded:

How it made me feel:

I am inspired to:

An act of kindness I saw today:

Additional Notes or Drawings:

DATE

TIME

Recipient:

What I did:

Why I did it:

How they responded:

How it made me feel:

I am inspired to:

An act of kindness I saw today:

Additional Notes or Drawings:

DATE

TIME

Recipient:

What I did:

Why I did it:

How they responded:

How it made me feel:

I am inspired to:

An act of kindness I saw today:

Additional Notes or Drawings:

DATE

TIME

Recipient:

What I did:

Why I did it:

How they responded:

How it made me feel:

I am inspired to:

An act of kindness I saw today:

DATE

TIME

Additional Notes or Drawings:

Recipient:

What I did:

Why I did it:

How they responded:

How it made me feel:

I am inspired to:

An act of kindness I saw today:

Additional Notes or Drawings:

DATE

TIME

Recipient:

What I did:

Why I did it:

How they responded:

How it made me feel:

I am inspired to:

An act of kindness I saw today:

DATE

TIME

Additional Notes or Drawings:

Recipient:

DATE
TIME

What I did:

Why I did it:

How they responded:

How it made me feel:

I am inspired to:

An act of kindness I saw today:

Additional Notes or Drawings:

Recipient:

DATE

What I did:

Why I did it:

TIME

How they responded:

How it made me feel:

I am inspired to:

An act of kindness I saw today:

Additional Notes or Drawings:

Recipient:

What I did:

Why I did it:

How they responded:

How it made me feel:

I am inspired to:

An act of kindness I saw today:

DATE

TIME

Additional Notes or Drawings:

Recipient:

What I did:

Why I did it:

How they responded:

How it made me feel:

I am inspired to:

An act of kindness I saw today:

DATE

TIME

Additional Notes or Drawings:

Recipient:

What I did:

Why I did it:

How they responded:

How it made me feel:

I am inspired to:

An act of kindness I saw today:

DATE

TIME

Additional Notes or Drawings:

Recipient:

What I did:

Why I did it:

How they responded:

How it made me feel:

I am inspired to:

An act of kindness I saw today:

Additional Notes or Drawings:

DATE

TIME

Recipient:

What I did:

Why I did it:

How they responded:

How it made me feel:

I am inspired to:

An act of kindness I saw today:

DATE

TIME

Additional Notes or Drawings:

Recipient:

What I did:

Why I did it:

How they responded:

How it made me feel:

I am inspired to:

An act of kindness I saw today:

Additional Notes or Drawings:

DATE

TIME

Recipient: _____

What I did: _____

Why I did it: _____

How they responded: _____

How it made me feel: _____

I am inspired to: _____

An act of kindness I saw today: _____

Additional Notes or Drawings:

DATE

TIME

Recipient:

What I did:

Why I did it:

How they responded:

How it made me feel:

I am inspired to:

An act of kindness I saw today:

DATE

TIME

Additional Notes or Drawings:

Recipient:

What I did:

Why I did it:

How they responded:

How it made me feel:

I am inspired to:

An act of kindness I saw today:

DATE

TIME

Additional Notes or Drawings:

Recipient:

What I did:

Why I did it:

How they responded:

How it made me feel:

I am inspired to:

An act of kindness I saw today:

DATE

TIME

Additional Notes or Drawings:

Recipient:

What I did:

Why I did it:

How they responded:

How it made me feel:

I am inspired to:

An act of kindness I saw today:

Additional Notes or Drawings:

DATE

TIME

Recipient:

What I did:

Why I did it:

How they responded:

How it made me feel:

I am inspired to:

An act of kindness I saw today:

DATE

TIME

Additional Notes or Drawings:

Recipient:

What I did:

Why I did it:

How they responded:

How it made me feel:

I am inspired to:

An act of kindness I saw today:

Additional Notes or Drawings:

DATE

TIME

Recipient:

What I did:

Why I did it:

How they responded:

How it made me feel:

I am inspired to:

An act of kindness I saw today:

DATE

TIME

Additional Notes or Drawings:

Recipient:

What I did:

Why I did it:

How they responded:

How it made me feel:

I am inspired to:

An act of kindness I saw today:

DATE

TIME

Additional Notes or Drawings:

Recipient:

What I did:

Why I did it:

How they responded:

How it made me feel:

I am inspired to:

An act of kindness I saw today:

DATE

TIME

Additional Notes or Drawings:

Recipient:

What I did:

Why I did it:

How they responded:

How it made me feel:

I am inspired to:

An act of kindness I saw today:

DATE

TIME

Additional Notes or Drawings:

Recipient:

What I did:

Why I did it:

How they responded:

How it made me feel:

I am inspired to:

An act of kindness I saw today:

Additional Notes or Drawings:

DATE

TIME

Recipient:

What I did:

Why I did it:

How they responded:

How it made me feel:

I am inspired to:

An act of kindness I saw today:

Additional Notes or Drawings:

DATE

TIME

Recipient:

DATE

What I did:

TIME

Why I did it:

How they responded:

How it made me feel:

I am inspired to:

An act of kindness I saw today:

Additional Notes or Drawings:

Recipient:

What I did:

Why I did it:

How they responded:

How it made me feel:

I am inspired to:

An act of kindness I saw today:

Additional Notes or Drawings:

DATE

TIME

Recipient:

What I did:

Why I did it:

How they responded:

How it made me feel:

I am inspired to:

An act of kindness I saw today:

Additional Notes or Drawings:

DATE

TIME

Recipient:

| DATE |
| TIME |

What I did:

Why I did it:

How they responded:

How it made me feel:

I am inspired to:

An act of kindness I saw today:

Additional Notes or Drawings:

Recipient:

What I did:

Why I did it:

How they responded:

How it made me feel:

I am inspired to:

An act of kindness I saw today:

DATE

TIME

Additional Notes or Drawings:

Recipient:

What I did:

Why I did it:

How they responded:

How it made me feel:

I am inspired to:

An act of kindness I saw today:

Additional Notes or Drawings:

DATE

TIME

Recipient:

What I did:

Why I did it:

How they responded:

How it made me feel:

I am inspired to:

An act of kindness I saw today:

DATE

TIME

Additional Notes or Drawings:

Recipient:

What I did:

Why I did it:

How they responded:

How it made me feel:

I am inspired to:

An act of kindness I saw today:

Additional Notes or Drawings:

DATE

TIME

Recipient:

What I did:

Why I did it:

How they responded:

How it made me feel:

I am inspired to:

An act of kindness I saw today:

Additional Notes or Drawings:

DATE

TIME

Recipient:

What I did:

Why I did it:

How they responded:

How it made me feel:

I am inspired to:

An act of kindness I saw today:

Additional Notes or Drawings:

DATE

TIME

Recipient:

What I did:

Why I did it:

How they responded:

How it made me feel:

I am inspired to:

An act of kindness I saw today:

DATE

TIME

Additional Notes or Drawings:

Recipient:

What I did:

Why I did it:

How they responded:

How it made me feel:

I am inspired to:

An act of kindness I saw today:

Additional Notes or Drawings:

DATE

TIME

Recipient:

What I did:

Why I did it:

How they responded:

How it made me feel:

I am inspired to:

An act of kindness I saw today:

DATE

TIME

Additional Notes or Drawings:

Recipient:

What I did:

Why I did it:

How they responded:

How it made me feel:

I am inspired to:

An act of kindness I saw today:

Additional Notes or Drawings:

DATE

TIME

Recipient:

What I did:

Why I did it:

How they responded:

How it made me feel:

I am inspired to:

An act of kindness I saw today:

DATE

TIME

Additional Notes or Drawings:

- Acts of Kindness Tracker -

- Acts of Kindness Tracker -

- Acts of Kindness Tracker -

- Acts of Kindness Tracker -

www.ingramcontent.com/pod-product-compliance
Lightning Source LLC
LaVergne TN
LVHW060332080526
838202LV00053B/4452